Fact Finders®

Teachers, that means Laugh Out Loud.
Yup, science can be Hilarious!

LOL Physical Science

The ATTRACTIVE TRUTH about MAGNETISM

by Jennifer Swanson
illustrated by Bernice Lum

Does anyone else find last names
with animals in them a little funny?
I mean, the author isn't really the
son of a swan.

Since we're on the subject of names,
what's a "bodzin" or a "lum?"

Consultant:
Alec Bodzin
Associate Professor of Science Education
Lehigh University
Bethlehem, Pennsylvania

CAPSTONE PRESS
a capstone imprint

Fact Finders are published by Capstone Press,
1710 Roe Crest Drive, North Mankato, Minnesota 56003.
www.capstonepub.com

Library of Congress Cataloging-in-Publication Data
Swanson, Jennifer.
The attractive truth about magnetism / by Jennifer Swanson ; illustrated by Bernice
Lum.
p. cm.—(Fact finders. LOL physical science)
Includes bibliographical references and index.
Summary: "Describes what magnetism is and how it works through humor and core
science content"—Provided by publisher.
Audience: Ages 10-12.
ISBN 978-1-4296-8603-7 (library binding) — ISBN 978-1-4296-9296-0 (paperback)
ISBN 978-1-62065-242-8 (ebook pdf)
1. Magnetism—Juvenile literature. 2. Magnets—Juvenile literature. I. Lum, Bernice,
ill. II. Title.
QC753.7.S93 2013
538—dc23   2012001750

Editorial Credits
Jennifer Besel, editor; Tracy Davies McCabe, designer; Svetlana Zhurkin, media
    researcher; Laura Manthe, production specialist

Photo Credits
Capstone Studio: Karon Dubke, 16, 29 (all); Getty Images: Simon Fraser (MRI), 27;
iStockphoto: alxpin, 5 (middle), 18, Talaj, back cover, 4, 32, Stacey Walker (frame),
cover and throughout; Library of Congress, 24; Shutterstock: Alis Leonte, 6 (back),
Andrea Danti (Earth), 7, April Cat, 10, archidea, 28 (back), Charlotte Erpenbeck
(background), cover and throughout, Diamond_Images (alphabet magnets), 5, Lee
Prince, 26, Margo Harrison (boxers), 27, mart (pencil scribbles), cover and throughout,
Olga Tropinina (arrows and speech bubbles), cover and throughout, Photo Grafix/
Black Rhino Illustration, 8 (back), pics721, 9 (back), Roman Krochuk, 19 (back),
s_oleg (painting), 5, SergeyIT, 13, Skyline (notebook sheet), cover and throughout,
Snowbelle, 7 (back), Steve Bower, 25 (middle), tuulijumala (explosion), 3 and
throughout, Vitaly Raduntsev (magnetite), 12

Printed in the United States of America in Brainerd, Minnesota
032012   006672BANGF12

TABLE (OF) CONTENTS

Title!

You have the power to push or pull objects without touching them. Your superpower even works through walls or water. All you need is courage ... and a really strong magnet.

OK, so you don't really have a superpower. But you do have super cool magnets that can do these things. Magnets use a force called magnetism. This invisible force allows magnets to **attract** or **repel** objects, just like a superhero.

Magnets are all around. They're in your TV and computer. You probably have one on the refrigerator to hold up your latest art project.

Or maybe it's holding up that test you didn't study for.

attract—to pull something toward something else
repel—to push apart

Magnetism is a power people use every day. Without it, TVs and cell phones wouldn't work. Even cars wouldn't go. Let's investigate this **FUN**damental force to see just how it works.

It's not just a necessary force. It's a fun force too! Magnetism is so cool.

5

Feel the Force

When you put two magnets near each other, you can feel a push or pull. The movement you feel is caused by a magnetic field. A magnetic field is an invisible area around an object. This field **exerts** a magnetic force that attracts or repels other objects. Magnetic fields look like curved lines around an object.

Metal objects are most sensitive to magnetic fields. Any metal object that comes into a magnetic field will be attracted to or repelled by the magnet.

Look at this magnetic field.

That is NOT the kind of field they're talking about.

The blue lines do not stand for football plays. They stand for Earth's magnetic field.

Magnetic fields are everywhere. In fact, even Earth acts like a very strong magnet. Deep in Earth's core, magnetism is created. The inner core is made of solid iron. The outer core is made of liquid iron and nickel. As the liquid iron moves around the solid iron, it creates an electric **current**. This electric current causes a magnetic field to form around the planet. So Earth is one giant magnet.

Try putting THAT on your fridge.

exert—to make an effort to do something
current—the flow of electrons

Polar Opposites

Just to be clear, this section has nothing to do with polar bears.

Every magnet has two parts—a north pole and a south pole. These poles are at opposite ends of a magnet. It's these opposite parts that determine if magnets attract or repel.

Just like you, magnetism always follows the rules.

You DO follow the rules, DON'T you?

Bring the north pole of a magnet toward the south pole of another magnet. The two will pull together almost immediately. But if you bring their north poles together, they push apart. This crazy push and pull is the magnetic force.

Sizing up the Shape

Magnets are not covered under the U.S. Constitution.

Not all magnets are created equal. Some are strong enough to pick up cars. Others are too weak to stick to the fridge. The strength of a magnet depends on three factors—size, shape, and material.

The size factor is pretty simple. Bigger magnets are stronger than smaller magnets. Easy peesy.

Shape affects a magnet's strength too. The closer a magnet's poles are to each other, the stronger its magnetic field. A bar magnet is a rectangular piece of iron. Bar magnets are not very strong. Their poles are far apart. Bar magnets are used in refrigerator magnets, **compasses**, and even as a way to close kitchen cabinets. The biggest bar magnet in the world is actually under your feet. Yep, Earth's core is a bar magnet.

But apple cores are not magnets. You can't use fruit to hang up your pictures. We tried. It only made applesauce all over the floor.

compass—an instrument people use to find the direction in which they are traveling

Another type of magnet is a horseshoe magnet. This type is much stronger than a bar magnet because its poles are closer. Horseshoe magnets are used at construction sites to pick up stray pieces of metal.

Although they are called horseshoe magnets, they were never used by horses. It's a good thing too. Could you imagine a horse walking across a steel bridge with magnetic shoes?

No horses were harmed in the fact-checking of this book.

I'm not horsing around here! I'm stuck.

What Are You Made Of?

A magnet's material also determines its strength. Some magnets are made of materials that are naturally magnetic. When a material is a natural magnet, it will magnetize metals that come near it. The mineral magnetite, also known as lodestone, is a natural magnet. These natural magnets are called permanent magnets.

I have a magnetic personality. I wear tights because that's the uniform of a hero. **I am Magnetite!**

OK, that's a stretch. But it's still a little funny.

When a metal comes in contact with a permanent magnet, it will become a magnet too. These types of magnets are called temporary magnets. Temporary magnets only behave as magnets when near other magnets.

Temporary bullies behave as bullies when near other bullies. Don't be like a temporary magnet ... or bully.

And now this book teaches character education too. Teachers, are you getting this?!

Chapter 2

What's Happenin'?

Magnetism begins between some of the tiniest things on Earth—atoms. Atoms are small pieces of matter that make up everything around us. Your computer, your backpack, even your hair is composed of atoms. They are so small you can't see them.

Every atom in a piece of metal acts like its own tiny magnet. The atoms are grouped together in domains. Each domain has its own north and south pole. Normally, the domains are pointed in random directions. Some have their north poles up and some have them down. But when the domains line up with each other, the piece of metal is magnetized.

This is exactly HOW zombies beHave. THey all go in ranDom Directions until a Human comes arounD. THen tHey line up like tHey're magnetizeD by tHe person's flesH. Maybe magnetism HolDs tHe key to stopping zombie attacks?!?!

Magnetization

before magnetization

after   N   S

Hold a bar magnet over a pile of paper clips. Almost immediately, the paper clips jump to the magnet. That's the movement you can see. But those tiny atoms in the paper clip were busy too. The domains in the metal paper clip were exposed to the magnet's magnetic field. The domains quickly lined up to be opposite to the field. Once that happened, the paper clip was magnetized and was attracted to the magnet.

Unless you are a superhero with mega-zooming sight powers. If you have that— WAY COOL!

What did the paper clip say to the magnet?

I find you very attractive.

Time for an Experiment!

So you read earlier about how permanent magnets can create temporary magnets. But did you know that you can make a magnet? It's as easy as one, two, three.

You read that on PAGE 13, didn't you?

1. **Get a magnet.**
2. **Get a piece of metal, such as iron or steel.**
3. **Rub the magnet over the metal several times, always in the same direction.**

With each stroke of the magnet, you align the metal's domains. Tah-dah!

You can actually make a compass with this method. Magnetize a sewing needle by rubbing from its eye to its point. Then poke it through a cork lengthwise. Float the cork in a glass of water and watch.

Really, you can. This compass really works. I DARE you to try it!

The needle will spin until it's aligned with Earth's magnetic field. The point will face Earth's magnetic north pole.

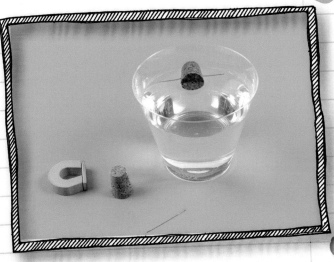

It does me no good to know where north is if I don't know where I'm going.

Losing It

The temporary magnets you made won't last forever. Over time, the domains shift. You can realign them just by using a permanent magnet on them again.

But can a permanent magnet lose its magnetic ability? Yes. If a permanent magnet is dropped from a distance or struck hard with a hammer, its domains could move. Heat can also affect magnetism. If a magnet gets too hot, then its domains may shift. When the domains shift they move out of alignment. The object is no longer magnetized.

Bummer.

Put Up the Shield!

Earth's magnetic field isn't just good for finding your way. The magnetic field lines around Earth stretch far out in space. They make up the **magnetosphere.** The magnetosphere is about 35,000 miles (56,327 kilometers) above Earth. There, Earth's magnetic forces play a big part in protecting the planet.

The Sun blows **particles** toward Earth at speeds of almost 1 million miles (1.6 million km) per second. Magnetosphere to the rescue! The sphere keeps those speeding particles from burning up the planet.

Sometimes I think scientists get lazy. I mean, couldn't they come up with a better name than magnetosphere? Sounds like where a comic book villain lives.

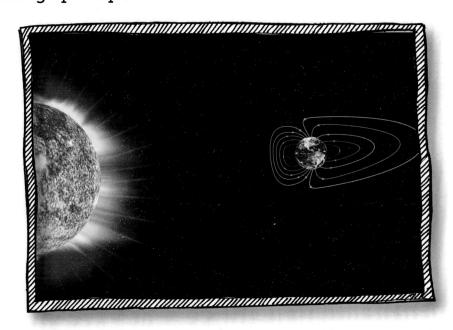

magnetosphere—the magnetic field extending into space around a planet
particle—a tiny piece of something

Wow! Could magnetism make my gases beautiful?

A few of the Sun's particles go through the magnetosphere into Earth's **atmosphere**. The particles spread out and interact with the atmosphere's gases. When this happens the particles glow. This glowing is known as the Aurora Borealis or the Northern Lights. Magnetism is beautiful!

I bet no other book on magnetism has said that before.

atmosphere—the mixture of gases that surrounds Earth

Chapter 3

A Little Shocking

Up until now you've read about pretty simple magnets. An object is either magnetized or it's not. However there is a type of magnet that can be turned on and off. But to make this magnet, you'll need to use the very same force that runs your refrigerator.

It might be shocking, but electricity and magnetism are closely related. Electricity works at the very smallest level of the atom. Inside atoms are electrons. They don't sit inside the nice cozy center of the atom. Electrons spin around the outside of an atom. Imagine the teacup ride at an amusement park. The center of the cup is like the center of the atom. The electrons would be on the edge of the cup, barely hanging on.

Sometimes the electrons fly off the cup. They leave one teacup for another. The movement of electrons from atom to atom is electricity.

Why is electricity so dangerous?
Because it can't conduct itself properly!

Did you get the joke? If not, you need to read up on electricity. We put info for the BEST electricity book on page 31 for you. You're welcome.

Don't try this yourself. You would not create electricity, although the results would be shocking.

When electricity flows through a wire, the movement creates a magnetic field. The magnetic force created by electricity is not very strong in one wire. But imagine a lot of wires wrapped around a piece of metal. Then run electricity through the wires. You get a very strong magnet called an electromagnet.

Here's the fun part. Electromagnets act just like regular magnets while the electricity is flowing. But when the electricity is turned off, the magnetism stops.

Ok, I know this isn't the best book you've ever read. But it's pretty good ... for a science book. Right?

Is this blowing your mind yet? I knew this would be the best book you've ever read. Tell your friends.

Gotta Go

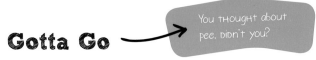

You thought about pee, didn't you?

Everything from doorbells to washing machines uses electromagnets. And they're in all motors and generators.

Motors have several parts. On the outside is a permanent magnet, called a field magnet. This magnet stays in place and does not move. The south pole of the magnet is on one side. The north end of the magnet is on the other.

Again, this has nothing to do with crops of any kind.

Inside the field magnet is an electromagnet. The electromagnet is attached to a bar called a commutator. The electromagnet's wire is hooked up to a battery or other energy source. When the electricity is turned on, the electromagnet has a magnetic field around it. The north pole of the electromagnet then attracts the south pole of the field magnet. As the two move together, the electromagnet turns.

You think of us every time you read "north pole" don't you?

Now comes the tricky part. Just as the electromagnet turns, the battery flips over. This flip changes the direction of the electrons in the wire. The north pole of the electromagnet becomes the south pole. Now you have two south poles repelling. The electromagnet turns again. Then the battery flips again. The constant switching of the magnetic field's direction causes the electromagnet to rotate.

As the electromagnet spins, it moves the commutator. The movement of the commutator can make a fan turn, a washing machine spin, or a drill rotate.

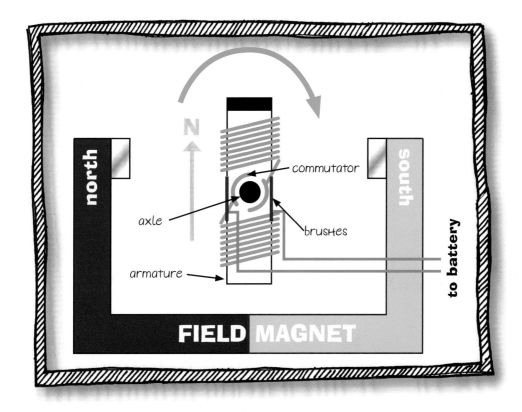

north

N

commutator

axle

brushes

armature

south

to battery

FIELD MAGNET

Generate Some Light

A motor uses electrical energy to create a magnetic force. But could you use a magnetic force to make electricity? You bet you can!

Making electricity from magnetism is done in a generator. A generator has all the same parts as a motor. It just works in the exact reverse order. In a generator the commutator must be turned by an outside force. Sometimes that force might be a hand crank. Remember seeing pictures of an old car with a hand crank? Someone had to turn the crank to start a generator that then started the car.

Stop looking at my butt, and look at the hand crank.

Generators are a very important part of our lives. They are used at power plants to provide electricity to our homes. A generator in a power plant burns coal or oil to make steam. The steam turns the commutator that gets the electromagnet going. Without the electromagnet attracting and repelling a field magnet, there wouldn't be electricity for your home.

I know your mom said your smile lights up a room. But she's wrong. Lightbulbs powered by magnetism and electricity do that. I'm sorry to burst your awesome bubble.

Joke Time!

How many wizards does it take to change a lightbulb?

It depends on what you want it to change into.

Way Cooler Than You Thought

So magnetism is a little more amazing than you thought, right? But wait—there's more.

The uses for magnetism continue to grow. Right now magnetism is being used in a new kind of high-speed train system. These trains are called maglev trains. Maglev is short for magnetic **levitation**. Here's how it works. A magnetized wire runs along the track. Large magnets under the train repel the track's wire. That repelling lifts the train more than 1 inch (2.5 cm) above the track. Then the wire uses a system of repelling and attracting to move the train along the track.

levitation—rising in the air and floating

Doctors use magnetism to help them figure out medical conditions too. You've heard of an MRI. Well, those letters stand for Magnetic Resonance Imagery. Yes, magnetic!!

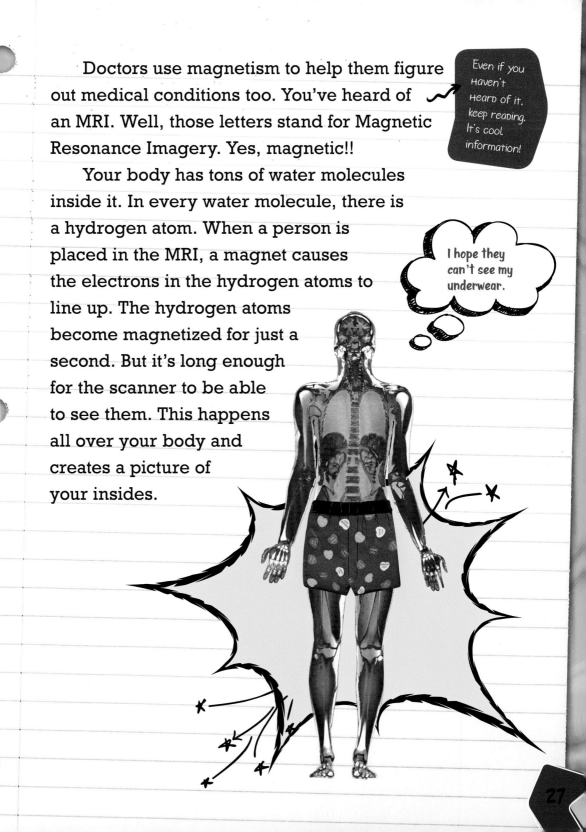

Even if you Haven't Heard of it, keep reading. It's cool information!

Your body has tons of water molecules inside it. In every water molecule, there is a hydrogen atom. When a person is placed in the MRI, a magnet causes the electrons in the hydrogen atoms to line up. The hydrogen atoms become magnetized for just a second. But it's long enough for the scanner to be able to see them. This happens all over your body and creates a picture of your insides.

I hope they can't see my underwear.

Magnetism is a powerful force. And people have only begun to understand all the ways it can be used. Right now magnets keep our phones working, our cars running, and our computers typing. Who knows what else could be done with a superpower like magnetism?

An important magnetic experiment:

OK, this isn't the most important thing that could be done with magnetism. But making a magnet dance is super cool!

Want to try? Get two round magnets that are about the size of quarters. Lay one on the table, and hold the other upright. Make sure the sides that repel are facing each other. Slowly slide the upright magnet toward the flat one, and watch it dance.

And that's the end. I know you're upset that it's over. But you can go back to the beginning and read it again. This book just has a magnetic quality. People just can't pull themselves away.

29

Glossary

atmosphere (AT-muhss-fihr)—the mixture of gases that surrounds Earth

attract (uh-TRAKT)—to pull something toward something else

compass (KUHM-puhs)—an instrument people use to find the direction in which they are traveling; a compass has a needle that points north

current (KUHR-uhnt)—the flow of electrons

exert (eg-ZURT)—to make an effort to do something

iron (EYE-urn)—a very hard metal

levitation (lev-i-TAY-shun)—rising in the air and floating

magnetosphere (mag-NET-oh-sfir)—the magnetic field extending into space around a planet or star

particle (PAR-tuh-kuhl)—a tiny piece of something

repel (ri-PEL)—to push apart; like poles of magnets repel each other

Read More

Goldsworthy, Kaite. *Magnetism.* Physical Science. New York: AV2 by Weigl, 2012.

Stewart, Melissa. *Shockingly Silly Jokes about Electricity and Magnetism.* Super Silly Science Jokes. Berkeley Heights, N.J.: Enslow Publishers, 2013.

Swanson, Jennifer. *The Shocking Truth about Electricity.* LOL Physical Science. North Mankato, Minn.: Capstone Press, 2013.

Internet Sites

FactHound offers a safe, fun way to find Internet sites related to this book. All of the sites on FactHound have been researched by our staff.

Here's all you do:

Visit *www.facthound.com*

Type in this code: 9781429686037

 **Super-cool stuff!** Check out projects, games and lots more at **www.capstonekids.com**

Index

Magnets are optimists. We always have a positive side.